Original title:
The Fruit of the Tropics

Copyright © 2025 Creative Arts Management OÜ
All rights reserved.

Author: Seraphina Caldwell
ISBN HARDBACK: 978-1-80581-578-5
ISBN PAPERBACK: 978-1-80581-105-3
ISBN EBOOK: 978-1-80581-578-5

## The Sway of Citrus Dreams

In a land where the lemons roll,
The oranges dance and take their toll.
Limes giggle, having a ball,
As monkeys throw cherries, oh what a call!

Papayas prance in a silly parade,
While the pineapples wear hats they've made.
Coconuts chuckle, swinging high,
And mangoes munch on clouds passing by.

Bananas slip in a playful sprawl,
With grapes that giggle and start to fall.
The guavas gossip, weaving their tales,
While the dragonfruit juggles without any fails.

Soursops sing in a kooky tune,
The starfruit spins like a wacky cartoon.
With a punch of color and laughter so sweet,
In this tropical circus, life is a treat!

## Bliss in every Bite

In a land where coconuts sway,
Palm trees dance the day away.
Mangoes drop in a juicy splat,
Watch out, or you'll wear that hat!

Pineapples wearing crowns so proud,
Make the squirrels giggle out loud.
Limes rolling like they stole the show,
Zesty jokes wherever you go!

## **Pulses of Paradise**

Bananas slip on sandy floors,
As laughter echoes from the shores.
Papayas lounging in the sun,
Whisper secrets, oh what fun!

Avocados thinking they're so cool,
Smooth and green, the tropical rule.
Coconuts shouting, "Crack me, please!"
Life is zany, and so full of ease!

## Flavors from Flora's Heart

Berries bouncing on leafy trails,
Tasting sunshine in their scales.
Mango lassis swirling wide,
Join the party, don't you hide!

Guavas giggling in the breeze,
Tart and sweet, if you please.
Rambutans with their hairy heads,
Wiggle-waggle on your spreads!

**Sweet Hues of Nature**

Watermelons splash in playful fights,
A juicy mess of pure delight.
Fruits parade in vibrant hues,
Tickling taste buds, singing blues!

Kiwis launch from branches high,
Landing squishy, oh my my!
Tropical jokes in every bite,
Snack with laughter, day or night!

## Paradise's Palette of Taste

In a land where giggles grow,
Mango hats in the sun's glow,
Banana peels do waltz and sway,
Limes throw parties every day.

Pineapples wear their crowns so high,
Coconuts laugh as they pass by,
Berries burst with bubbly cheer,
While papayas dance without a fear.

**Dances of the Tropical Orchard**

Guavas twist, with a shake and spin,
Twirling away from a pesky pin,
Oranges juggle on a breezy day,
While cherries come out to laugh and play.

Lemons leaping, what a sight,
Tasting sweet while being bright,
Kiwis in a conga line,
All unite for a fruity rhyme.

## The Sizzle of Sunshine

Underneath the fiery ball,
Papayas roll and mangoes sprawl,
Watermelons jumping on their seeds,
While cherries giggle in the breeze.

Lemonade rivers flow with glee,
All the fruits sing in harmony,
Coconuts crack with joyous clinks,
Lost in laughter, what everyone thinks!

## Juicy Journeys

On a bus made of fresh kiwi,
Pineapples travel oh so freely,
Every stop bursts with sweet delight,
As tropical treats take a flight.

In the sky, with clouds of cream,
Fruits engage in a playful dream,
Riding breezes of warm delight,
As laughter spills from day to night.

## A Taste of Paradise

In a land where coconuts spin,
Laughter bubbles like sweet gin.
Bananas wear their brightest grin,
Dancing 'round like they're on vim.

Papayas jump with childlike glee,
Swaying gently, oh can't you see?
Oranges giggle on the tree,
Mixing joy with a splash of spree.

## Juicy Secrets of the Isle

Pineapples wear their crowns so proud,
Underneath, they yell aloud:
'We're the kings of the fruiting crowd!'
Gather round, we're juice endowed.

Mangoes whisper tales at dusk,
As they blend, they're simply tusk.
With their sweetness, it's a must,
Join this feast, it's a fruit-funk rust!

## Melodies of Mango and Pineapple

Mangoes sing a sunny tune,
While pineapples shake to the moon.
Bananacasters join in soon,
A fruit band, like none too ruin.

Limes are crooning, oh so sly,
Their zesty notes, they won't deny.
Dancing fruit, we can't see why,
A fruity party, let's say bye!

## Garden of the Sun's Embrace

In this garden, fruits collide,
Dancing under sunshine wide.
Grapefruit laughs, and so does pride,
With every slice, we share the ride.

Lychee winks, a mystery sweet,
Tropical rhythm, can't be beat.
Their juicy antics keep the beat,
In sun's embrace, all are replete.

## Tropical Serenade

In a land where pineapples wear hats,
And coconuts dance with the chitchat,
Mangoes giggle as they swing on trees,
While bananas play tag with the buzzing bees.

Papayas wiggle, full of delight,
Under the sun, they sparkle so bright.
Laughter echoes, as fruits frolic and sway,
In this silly paradise, all night and all day.

## Lush Bounty of the Sun

Lemons squirt jokes with a zesty grin,
Oranges mime with a pirouette spin.
Lemons yell, 'Hey, get in my drink!'
While limes roll over, all in good sync.

Guavas gossip, causing a stir,
Cherries twirl, giving the world a blur.
A fruity fiesta, what a sight to see,
Where watermelons juggle with glee and esprit.

## Whispers in the Palm Groves

In the shadows where shadows become pals,
Coconuts write memoirs of silly gales.
Pineapples plot in a secretive tone,
While papayas pull pranks, never alone.

The winds carry giggles, swaying along,
As berries create their most awkward song.
Laughter springs forth from every leafy end,
In the palm groves where humor will blend.

## Nectar of the Evening Breeze

Strawberries wear sunglasses, basking so fine,
As grapes drop beats, making rhythms divine.
Under the glow of a silly moonlight,
Fruits share secrets, all through the night.

Kiwis play hopscotch on sandy shores,
While dragonfruits whisper their ancient lores.
In this comedy, the sun takes a bow,
As the fruits teach us to laugh, here and now.

## Fruits Beneath the Palms

Under palm fronds, a wacky sight,
Coconuts plummet in broad daylight.
Mangoes slide by in their juicy glee,
While bananas giggle, "Look at me!"

Pineapples wear their crowns so proud,
While papayas dance in the sun-baked crowd.
Limes crack jokes, lemons roll their eyes,
Tropical humor beneath sunny skies.

## Luscious Tastes of Warm Winds

In the breeze, ripe fruits take flight,
Guavas whisper, "Try our delight!"
With each bite, a chuckle reveals,
Peculiar flavors, oh what a meal!

Jackfruit jests, "Guess my weight!"
While mingling with strangers, they create fate.
Passion fruit winks, teasing with zest,
Eating here feels like a jest!

## **Sunkissed Harvest Moon**

Under the moon, fruits don their glow,
Tangerines twinkle, putting on a show.
Under starry backdrop, laughter rounds,
Hilarity blooms in the orchard grounds.

Lychee giggles, all silky and sweet,
Kicking back, taking off their suite.
As bananas start their salsa dance,
Fruits unite in a merry prance!

## Harvests from the Heart of Nature

Nature's laughter fills the air,
Fruits cracking jokes without a care.
Oranges toss puns in the sun,
While cherries giggle—it's all in fun!

Pomegranates spill secrets, juicy and bold,
Tropical tales of treasures untold.
So let's share a smile, maybe a bite,
In this world of sweetness, everything's right!

## Flavorful Journeys

I took a trip to the land of sauce,
Where pineapples wear hats, and lemons may douse.
Mangoes start dancing on tables with cheer,
While coconuts gossip that no one can hear.

Bananas in pajamas go slipping around,
Chasing each other, they bounce on the ground.
In this wacky place where smoothies take flight,
Every sip's an adventure, a taste bud delight.

## The Colors of Abundance

Orange with envy, lime looking green,
Blueberries grinning, a sweet berries scene.
Peaches are blushing like they've had too much sun,
While cherries are busy making jokes just for fun.

Grapes throw confetti, a fruity parade,
Watermelons juggling, watch them invade!
Every bite's a giggle, a tasty explosion,
In this vibrant world, there's pure fruity devotion.

**Tropical Whirlwind**

In a blender, a chaos, a swirl and a toss,
Bananas and kiwis, all dancing like bosses.
Mangoes do the limbo, papayas join in,
Throw in some ice, let the carnival begin!

Pineapples prank call, "Hey, is this a fruit stand?"
Guavas are laughing, taking selfies so grand.
The blender whirs loudly, a riot of fun,
In this whirlwind of flavor, who's winning? Everyone!

## Rhythms of the Fruit-bearing Trees

Under the canopy where laughter is heard,
Bouncing coconuts fly, it's truly absurd!
Papayas are playing a raucous old tune,
While starfruit sings softly beneath the full moon.

Avocados are grooving, they sway to the beat,
As oranges shuffle and tap their round feet.
In this leafy dance floor, a party unfolds,
With fruity festivities, pure joy it beholds!

## Flavors of Forgotten Islands

In a land where pineapples wear hats,
Mangoes trade gossip with chatty cats.
Coconuts bounce in a lively game,
While papayas argue over a name.

Tamarind sneezes, the guavas all laugh,
Bananas dance, trying to find their path.
Under the sun, they frolic and play,
While oranges giggle, brightening the day.

## Sun-Soaked Whimsy

A berry roller coaster, what a sight,
Limes doing flips, with pure delight.
Lychees swing from tropical vines,
As every fruit juggles, sipping on wines.

Coconut shells serve drinks with a cheer,
While passionfruit whispers secrets in your ear.
Grapefruits kite-flying, soaring so high,
While avocados just wave as they pass by.

## Ode to the Tropical Orchard

In the grove, a watermelon sings,
Twirling with joy, oh the joy it brings.
Pineapple struts with a crown on its head,
And coconuts giggle as they roll off the bed.

Dragonfruits paint murals on the ground,
While citrus showers spread laughter around.
Fruits in pajamas, lounging in the sun,
In this orchard world, everyone's having fun!

## Wordless Wonders Among the Leaves

In the forest, a lychee wore small shoes,
Dancing with limes, breaking all the news.
Mangoes trade jokes, full of zest,
While bananas nap, clearly feeling blessed.

The durian grins, it knows it's unique,
While rambutan shares a laugh, cheek to cheek.
Under leafy canopies, mischief blooms,
With all kinds of laughter filling the rooms.

## Exotic Flavors in Bloom

When mangoes leap like frogs in rain,
And pineapples wear sunglasses for the gain,
The coconut does a salsa dance,
While papayas giggle, given half a chance.

Bananas play peek-a-boo from their trees,
Oranges throw parties, aiming to please,
Kiwi comes in, all fuzzy and bright,
Says, "Join the fun, I'm ready for a bite!"

## Coral Gardens of Taste

In a sea of flavors where coconuts float,
Passionfruit sings, wearing a colorful coat,
Limes throw confetti, soda's their song,
Berries in bows cheer, "Come join our throng!"

The starfruit winks, quite sure of its charm,
While guavas gossip without any harm,
Tasting adventures in vibrant cuisine,
A buffet of laughter, a fruity routine!

## Sweet Symphony of the Tropics

Behold the orchestra with fruit as its crew,
The durian sighs, sweet perfumes breezing through,
Lychee hits high notes, all juicy and round,
As jackfruit strums bass, a deep, bumpy sound.

The tamarind teases, a sour little troll,
With a twist of charisma, playing its role,
Bananas harmonize, in yellow delight,
Creating tunes that dance well into night!

## Island Abundance

On sandy shores where the fruit trees sway,
Coconut waters serve drinks every day,
Mango slices frolic, spritzed with a swirl,
While spicy chili peppers give a twirl.

Avocado lounges, so smooth and so green,
Says, "Join me, my friends, for a dip that's serene!"
The festival's here, so bring out your grin,
In this paradise, let the fun begin!

## Exotic Tastings from Above

In the jungle, fruits are sweet,
Bananas dance with eager feet.
Mangoes wink from leafy shade,
Coconut jokes that never fade.

Papayas giggle, all in bloom,
Pineapples wear a spiky costume.
Guavas play hide and seek with bees,
As laughter floats upon the breeze.

Lychee's blush, a cheeky tease,
Rambutan's hair blows in the breeze.
Cherries huddle for a chat,
All the fruits know where it's at!

Between the laughs and fruity chats,
Savoring bites, we all lose stats.
So come and join this lively crew,
And munch on joy, just me and you!

**Slices of Serenity**

In the sun, a slice of glee,
Watermelon sings with me.
Lemonade smiles, tart and true,
While oranges juggle out of view.

Papaya shares a silly grin,
As friendliest mango swings on in.
In this patch of laughter bright,
Fruits take the stage, a pure delight.

Bananas split with laughter loud,
While grapes declare they're feeling proud.
On a picnic blanket spread,
Fruity games, forget your dread.

Chill vibes shimmer in the sun,
With every slice, we laugh and run.
So bring your joy, unwrap a treat,
These slices make our day complete!

**Dreams in Color**

In a dream where colors splash,
Fruits come alive with a vibrant bash.
Red strawberries frolic in the sun,
While leafy greens chase just for fun.

Blueberries burst like happy tunes,
Singing sweet songs beneath the moons.
Orange slices do a crazy twist,
While laughing grapes can't be missed!

Each berry wears a colorful hat,
While kiwi spins and does a splat.
In this world, joy takes the lead,
Each fruit invites you, take a heed!

With every bite, a giggle bloomed,
In dreams of color, we are all groomed.
Join this feast, don't hesitate,
These fruity dreams can't wait for fate!

## Currents of Freshness

Fruits float down a river wide,
Juicy secrets, they can't hide.
Splashing berries, bright as day,
In fruity currents, we find our way.

Limes twist and turn with flair,
While cooled bananas show off hair.
Mangoes high-five in the stream,
With every splash, we laugh and beam.

Coconut boats on waves so free,
Carrying joy for you and me.
Pineapples surf on fruity tide,
In this freshness, we take pride!

So let's dive deep and have some fun,
This fruity party has just begun!
With every sip, our worries fade,
In currents of freshness, we're unafraid!

## Harvest Moon in Paradise

Under a moon so round and bright,
Coconuts dance in the soft moonlight.
The laughter flows like mangoes sweet,
As folks juggle fruits and shuffle their feet.

Pineapples wear hats, oh what a sight,
While avocados argue who's heavier tonight.
We toast with papayas, cheers in the breeze,
In this paradise, laughter is the key!

## Juices of the Wilds

Sipping on drinks that glow and fizz,
With flavors that strange, yet are always a whiz.
Limes make faces, and kiwis sing,
While unicorns dance, it's a magical fling!

The berries compete in a juicy race,
With oranges claiming the zesty space.
Mangoes slip on their rinds, oh dear!
Who knew wilds could be this full of cheer!

## Splashes of Tropical Rain

Raindrops drip like syrupy bliss,
While bananas slide in a juicy kiss.
Tropical showers bringing giggles galore,
Fruit party starts, who could ask for more!

Coconuts toss in a splashy dance,
Papayas twirl in a watery prance.
When the sky pours down a fruity song,
We all join in, can't help but sing along!

## **Bananas and Bliss**

Bananas in pajamas doing a jig,
While mangos bring laughter, all big and swig.
In a bowl of fruit salad, they all have a ball,
Making friends with berries, both short and tall.

With every munch, there's giggles and cheer,
Even grapes in a bunch, feeling quite clear.
Life's a treat with this fruity crew,
If you're feeling low, just blend one or two!

**Tropic's Vibrant Palette**

Sunshine whispers, colors glow,
Banana peels in a funny show.
Mangoes dance, a juicy mime,
Lime giggles, sharing limey rhyme.

Coconuts with hidden charms,
Bounce around, causing alarms.
Papayas sing with laughing glee,
In this land of fruity spree.

Every hue a playful tease,
Bouncing like the ocean breeze.
With each bite, a smile's birthed,
Tropic's joke, the sweetest mirth.

## Secrets in the Shade of Palms

Underneath the velvet sky,
Lemons giggle, oh my, oh my!
Pineapples wear their prickly hats,
Cracking jokes with sassy sprats.

Fruits hide secrets, sly as can be,
In the shade, let's sip fruity tea.
Kiwi whispers, "I'm quite bold,
Want to hear my tale retold?"

Coconut smiles beneath its shell,
"I'm not just a hard-knock shell!"
Mischief brews in every bite,
Tropical laughter, pure delight.

## Melon Medley of the Islands

Watermelon in a striped suit,
Claims to be the fanciest fruit.
Honeydew, with a winking eye,
Says, "I'm sweeter, oh my, oh my!"

Cantaloupe joins the banter bold,
Laughs with laughter that's never old.
They play games in the summer heat,
Rolling around, oh what a treat!

Juicy smiles as they slide on by,
In this fruity showdown, oh my!
Every slice tells a funny tale,
Melons rule the tropical trail!

## Sweets of the Subtropics

Cherries giggle on their vine,
Sassy pouts, a fruit divine.
Figs dance with a fruity flair,
Whispers sweet in the tropical air.

Guavas prance in vibrant hues,
Trading outfits just for views.
Jackfruit teases, "Look at me!
I'm the star of this fruity spree!"

Lemon drops from citrus trees,
Sings a tune with playful ease.
Tropical party, what a scene,
Sweets abound, the best cuisine!

## Citrusy Dreams Beneath the Canopy

Under zesty skies, lemons roll,
Limes laugh, their jokes take a toll.
Oranges giggle, wearing their hue,
While grapefruits guess what we'll do.

Beneath leafy shades, the fruits play tag,
With swinging vines, each fruit does brag.
Bananas slip with a big ol' grin,
Saying, "Join us in this fruity din!"

Mangoes sway to a rhythmic beat,
While coconuts offer a spa retreat.
Chilling vibes under the sun's embrace,
It's a citrus party, come join the race!

## Harvest of Vibrant Delights

In a bright bazaar, berries collide,
Fruits dressed in chaos, let's take a ride.
Cherry bombs bounce, causing a cheer,
Pineapples wink, "We're all friends here!"

With every bite, there's a funny twist,
Passion fruits giggle, there's no way to resist.
"Let's salsa dance!" the melons proclaim,
As guavas laugh, bringing no shame.

Kiwis hide midst their fuzzy attire,
While figs joke that they're the bonfire.
Epic parade of tastes intertwined,
In this harvest, pure joy we find!

## The Papaya's Dance

In a bright grove, a papaya swayed,
With rhythm so smooth, it's never delayed.
"Look at me dance!" it called with a cheer,
While zestful limes burst from the rear.

Dressed in orange, a sight to behold,
Twisting and turning, never too bold.
With a wink to a mango, it said with a grin,
"Join in the fun, let's get it on, kin!"

Avocados chuckled, not wanting to miss,
"Let's make a smoothie!" they couldn't resist.
The tropics exploded in laughter and song,
As the papaya led the fruit parade along.

## **Sweet Reverie in the Tropics**

In sunny days of fruity delight,
Ripe bananas giggle, causing a fright.
Coconut's laughter fills the warm air,
"Who needs a helmet when you've got hair?"

Pineapples sport crowns, feeling so royal,
While berries take turns to spin, being loyal.
"Let's make a jam!" they cheerfully shout,
Ripe with laughter, they dance about.

A fruity fiesta, each taste buds unite,
Mangoes and dragon fruits causing a light.
In a sweet reverie, joy never ends,
These tropical dreams are lifelong friends!

## Oasis of Flavors

In a land where pineapples dance,
Coconuts wear a hula pants,
Mangoes giggle, ripe and sweet,
Bananas slip in a funny seat.

Parrots squawk with fruity cheer,
While a lime rolls away in fear,
A papaya starts to break a joke,
As passion fruits begin to poke.

The sun shines bright in a silly way,
Watermelons plan a beach day,
Tropical breeze makes peaches sway,
Join this feast, come out and play!

Orange slices on a sunny plate,
Everyone laughing, it's just great,
In this oasis of zest and fun,
Life's a party for everyone!

## Melodies of the Jungle

In the jungle where the berries sing,
Monkeys jump, imagining spring,
Kiwi birds with their silly calls,
Wrinkled praise for the fruit walls.

Grapefruits wear their hats askew,
Twitching leaves say, how do you do?
While chili peppers dance with grace,
And cherries blush, oh what a place!

The forest hums with laughter loud,
A cocktail mix makes the fruits proud,
Lemurs laugh at the sly old fox,
While grapes play hopscotch with the rocks.

Coconuts play the bongo beat,
In jungle fun, there's no defeat,
A fruity concert, come take a look,
Grab your friends for this funny book!

## Tropic's Sweet Serenade

Under the palms with a sweet surprise,
Pineapples chat under bright skies,
Limes roll down in a comical race,
While bananas split with a giggling face.

Citrus dreams in a vibrant chat,
Don't be surprised if a mango acts fat,
Berries tease with their juicy flair,
While a coconut shimmies without a care.

The rhythm of fruit starts to flow,
Avocados swing to and fro,
Papayas croon with a fruity twist,
In this tornadic, tasty tryst.

Laughter echoes on the warm shore,
Each bite brings joy and so much more,
In this serenade, take a chance,
Join the fruit in a jolly dance!

## **Colors of Tropical Fields**

Painted fields of vibrant hues,
Fruits parade in lavish shoes,
Fuzzy peaches strut around,
While yellow lemons tumble down.

Raspberries giggle, trying to hide,
Amongst the greens, where coconuts bide,
A pomelo rolls, feeling quite grand,
As the banana crew makes a stand.

Tropical colors burst like confetti,
Where every fruit feels nice and petty,
Cherries chuckle in their bright red glow,
In fields of fun, there's always a show.

So come and dance in the sunny light,
With fruits so happy, it feels just right,
In this carnival of flavors, be bold,
The colors of joy are waiting to unfold!

## A Symphony of Seasons

In a garden where laughter grows,
Mangos dance with their yellow toes.
Coconuts tumble, what a sight,
Pineapples giggle, oh what delight!

Papayas swing from the leafy arms,
While bananas flex their fruity charms.
A fruit fiesta all around,
Where every bite is joy unbound.

Melons roll with a cheeky grin,
Berries blush, let the fun begin!
Each fruity friend joins the spree,
In this orchard of jubilee!

Limes wear shades, looking so cool,
Oranges bounce like they're in school.
The tropics sing with a cheerful play,
In this fruity jamboree every day!

## Orchard under the Moonlight

Under the moon, fruit twirls and sways,
Lemons laugh in their zesty ways.
Kiwi zips on its fuzzy feet,
As starfruit organizes a fleet.

Coconut whispers secrets low,
While guavas start a late-night show.
Rambutans with their wild, weird hair,
Invite all the fruits to dance in the air.

Beneath the stars, a juicy ball,
Cherries bounce and begin to sprawl.
Tropical tunes fill the night,
With every bite, the world feels right.

Laughter echoes, fruity delight,
In this orchard, hearts take flight.
When the moon shines bright like a score,
The fruits unite, who could ask for more?

## Lush Landscapes and Ripe Reveries

In the fields where the colors pop,
Fruits in rows ready to swap.
Pineapples wear tart crowns with flair,
While cherries laugh, tossing in the air.

Guavas sway with a playful breeze,
Bantam bananas shimmy with ease.
Watermelons rolling down the hill,
Creating the fruity fun-filled thrill!

Peaches parade in their fuzzy coats,
While kumquats cheer in little boats.
Avocados dreaming of a toast,
Throw a party, let's raise a boast!

Tropical fruits, a colorful crew,
Join the fun, there's room for you!
In this landscape, wild and bright,
Every moment is pure delight.

## Elysium of the Evergreen

In evergreen halls where fruits abound,
Oranges gossip without a sound.
Papayas wear laughter like a cloak,
As nutty coconuts tell a joke.

Avocados, smooth and in a line,
Invite all fruits to dine and dine.
Luscious laughter fills the balmy air,
Each ripe friend is beyond compare.

Wild berries tease, their sweet-tart bite,
While grapefruits roll, looking quite bright.
Citrus serenades the blissful eve,
In this paradise, who can believe?

Under leaves, where fun never wane,
Fruits play games and dance in the rain.
Life's a feast, a tasty spree,
A tropical party, oh so free!

## Flavorful Fires of the Tropical Sun

When coconuts dance on the beach,
Bikinis giggle at mango's reach.
Pineapple hats on silly heads,
All laughing while sipping sweet spreads.

The papaya skies burst in cheer,
Lemons roll down with no sense of fear.
Chasing limes on a sun-soaked spree,
These fruits know how to throw a party!

Passion fruits plotting a splash,
Tropic breeze plays a silly sash.
Bananas slip in a playful race,
Citrus smiles on each joyful face.

Guava sings with a quirky sound,
Dancing with rhythms all around.
Adventure baked in the tropical fun,
Under the flavorful fires of the sun!

## Harvesting Harmony

In a field where starfruit gleams,
Silly squirrels plot fruity schemes.
Watermelon seats for a few,
Sharing giggles with a sweet view.

Coconut clinks in a playful fight,
Fruits dash left, then dash right.
Berries burst in laugh-out-loud,
Mischief bubbling, ripe and proud.

Every bite is a burst of cheer,
Laughter echoes, no hint of fear.
Snacking on laughter and silly smiles,
Fruits unite in whimsical styles.

Dancing grapes in a fruity trance,
Inviting everyone for a chance.
Harvesting joy as the sun dips low,
Savoring sweetness in a vibrant show!

## The Honeyed Horizon

The horizon drips with nectar dreams,
Giggling bees join fruity teams.
Mangoes gather in a chatty row,
Swapping stories as breezes blow.

Lychee lollipops twirl in delight,
While bananas swap shoes and take flight.
Papaya whispers its secrets high,
As coconuts roll with a happy sigh.

A horizon painted in zesty hues,
Cheeky laughter, no hint of blues.
Oranges juggle with cheeky flair,
Under the sun with fruity flair.

Every sunset tells a funny tale,
As clouds of cotton candy sail.
Nature giggles with colors wide,
In a honeyed horizon, joy can't hide!

## Nature's Opulent Arsenal

Nature's stash is a treasure chest,
With bananas dressed to the nines, no less.
Orchards filled with a quirky crew,
Cultivating fun with every hue.

A stash of berries in frolicsome displays,
Crafting smiles in curious ways.
Coconuts, bananas, and a zesty lime,
Watch them square off in a playful climb.

Fruits in a joyous secret race,
No one wins, but all find their place.
In laughter's garden, they spread delight,
Nature's bounty shining so bright.

Each fruity friend with a story to share,
Swinging through moments without a care.
An arsenal of joy so rich and sweet,
Nature's gift, a whimsical treat!

## Spirited Splendor in Every Slice

A pineapple wearing shades, so bright,
Sips on coconut until the night.
Mangoes dance, in tropical glee,
Swaying to rhythms beneath a palm tree.

Bananas slip on a colorful slide,
Chasing passion fruits with joyful pride.
Lemons grin, throwing tart little jibes,
While lychees gossip in juicy tribes.

Kiwi is the jester in a hat,
With a pear saying, "What's up with that?"
Avocados roll their eyes in delight,
As guavas tell tales of last night's flight.

Life is a picnic, laughter in air,
With cheeky fruits, there's mischief to share.
Every slice brings a giggle and cheer,
In this garden of humor, we persevere.

## Nectarine Dreams Beneath Tropical Skies

Under blue blankets where laughter reigns,
Nectarines throw parties without any chains.
Papayas wear hats made of plump leaves,
Dreaming of voyages, oh how it weaves!

Jackfruit tells tales taller than trees,
While cherries cheer with a pop and a squeeze.
Coconuts wobble, dancing all day,
Claiming that summer is here to stay.

Each fruit is a character, free to explore,
Passion fruit jumps, shouting, "I want more!"
Bananas play pranks, they're slippery bold,
Tea serpents giggle in vines, uncontrolled.

A fiesta of flavors in glorious fun,
With laughter and juice 'til the day is done.
Under the sun, in this fruity parade,
We mix all our joy, let the good times cascade.

## Blessings of the Jungle Orchard

In the jungle, bananas audition for fame,
While grapefruits giggle, no pulse, no shame.
Crawdads float by in a berry brigade,
Whispering secrets that sunlight portrayed.

Tangerines chuckle, their voices so sweet,
As melons stretch wide, share spa-like retreat.
Papaws share dreams of adventures at sea,
While limes sneak a sip of the wild jubilee.

Avocados debate who's the best-looking slice,
In a peck of bananas, they roll the dice.
With juicy gossip that ripens with age,
Every fruit flaunts its colorful stage.

Blessings abound in this jungle so green,
With each fruity shenanigan, laughter is seen.
Here in this orchard, mischief is grand,
A joyful embrace, hand in hand.

## Bounty from the Breezy Isles

From breezy isles, a parade on the shore,
Where coconuts gossip and oranges roar.
Kiwis are sunbathing, basking in sun,
Beneath laughing clouds, oh, isn't it fun?

Flamingo fruit cocktails with cherries on top,
Cresting waves of laughter, they never will stop.
Pineapple floats by in a surfboard of dreams,
While bananas compete in daring extremes.

Soursop grins widely, a captivating face,
While starfruits chart courses, a wild race.
In this sunny refuge, mirth shines so bright,
With colors that pop, it's a sheer delight.

So raise your glass full of fruity cheer,
Celebrate life with friends far and near.
In this island bounty, where grins never cease,
Every sip, every slice, brings joy and peace.

## Threads of Flavor through Warm Days

Beneath the sun, a feast awaits,
Mango dances on my plate.
Pineapple plays the ukulele,
While papaya giggles gaily.

Coconut laughs with a shifty grin,
As I drench in juice, soaking in.
Bananas swing from shady trees,
Throwing peels down with the breeze.

Limes are sour, yet make me smile,
Chasing them down, they run a mile.
Guava winks, then takes a dive,
What a way to feel alive!

Sipping fruit punch, I start to sway,
Dancing wildly through the day.
Tropical ruckus, oh what fun,
In this fruity place, I've surely won!

## The Artistry of Island Fare

Art on a plate, oh what a sight,
Pasta with mango takes flight.
Avocado paints a creamy scene,
While chili cheeks blush a vibrant green.

Shrimp in coconuts, what a blend,
A sea-salt serenade to attend.
Watermelon heads roll with glee,
They're the life of this fruity spree!

Chili peppers in a dance-off,
With sweet guava giving a scoff.
Tart and sweet, these flavors collide,
Creating joy I can't hide.

Hands up high, it's a fiesta,
Each bite's a laugh, a true siesta.
In this paradise, laughter's our guide,
Artistry served, oh what a ride!

## Cradled by Ferns and Citron

In a cradle of ferns, I find my seat,
With juicy citrus, oh what a treat!
Lemons jive with chubby limes,
Squeezing joy in fruity rhymes.

Trees lean in, gossiping cheer,
Rambutan shouts, 'Come over here!'
Dragons fruit with a spiky grin,
Invites me in for a fruity spin.

Papyrus waves with playful glee,
As I munch this zesty spree.
The tartness tickles, the sweet bites charm,
Wrapped in ferns, what a warm balm!

Colors burst, making me dance,
In this Eden, I take a chance.
Cradled here, I let out a shout,
With laughter and fruits, there's never a doubt!

## The Allure of Ripe Extravagance

Jungle vibes and laughter pair,
Melons roll without a care.
Durians flirt with a pungent tease,
Making noses crinkle with ease.

Cherries giggle, swaying on top,
While lychee smiles, "Come take a pop!"
Bouncing berries, full of cheer,
Whispering secrets that only we hear.

Passions burst with a juicy smack,
Flavors twist on a fruity track.
A papaya surprise, a pineapple spin,
This tropical ride is a win-win!

So come take a seat, join the fun,
In this orchard where laughter's spun.
Extravagance ripe, in perfect array,
In this merry plant party, we'll sway!

## Mosaic of Tropical Tastes

In a land where pineapples dance,
Mangoes waltz in a juicy trance.
Coconuts chuckle from trees so tall,
While papayas giggle and bounce like a ball.

Bananas wear spots as cool as a cat,
Limes give wedgies—now imagine that!
Peaches pout while oranges tease,
All partying under the coconut leaves.

The berries bicker, a raucous crew,
Each one claiming it's the best, boo-hoo!
With flavors so bright, it's a carnival fun,
In this zany patch, there's room for everyone!

When the sun sets low, what a sight to see,
A fruit fiesta, wild as can be.
With laughter and joy, they sing their song,
In this tropical land, where all belong!

# Orchard Drawn by the Winds

A breeze blew in with a mischievous grin,
Whispers of sweetness, let the feast begin.
Fruits loop-de-loop in the vibrant sun,
What a wild party; oh, this is fun!

Guavas giggle, guavas shout,
Dragon fruits prance, doing a roundabout.
But watch out for avocados, they're sly!
Lurking in shadows, they think they can fly.

Lemons are tossing their zesty jokes,
While cherries burst out in giggling croaks.
An orchard alive with faces so bright,
Every bite's a punchline, pure delight!

Under the moon, the flavors collide,
With laughter and joy, there's no need to hide.
A whirlwind of tastes in a hilarious spins,
In this wild garden, everybody wins!

## Embrace of the Lush

In the embrace of the ever-green,
Fruits are flaunting a show so keen.
Lush and plump, they wiggle and sway,
As the sun blinks down at the silly play.

Kiwi pulls faces, what a goofy sight,
Pineapples wear crowns—oh, what a height!
Citrus sisters all laugh and roll,
While rib-tickling cherries steal the whole show!

The orchards resound with sweet, cheeky glee,
As coconuts snicker in jovial spree.
Papaya's in costume, an odd little sight,
Wearing a peel and laughing outright!

In this haven of laughter, let's raise a toast,
To fruit in their prime, each one a boast.
With chuckles and nibbles, we'll savor each bite,
Under the sun's glow, everything feels right!

## Cravings of the Coast

By the shore where the wild waves play,
Tropical treasures are here to stay.
Fruits in baskets, what a sight to behold,
Like gems of the ocean, both spicy and bold!

Coconuts roll like they lost the race,
While starfruits shimmer, a fruity embrace.
Berries in hats, they dance in the sand,
With laughter erupting, it's all well-planned!

Mangoes in limbo, twisting with flair,
Bananas say, 'Hey! We want some air!'
The beach is a buffet, so ripe with fun,
A feast for the senses, we've just begun!

As the sun dips low, colors in flight,
With chatter and laughter, every delight.
In this crazy coast, where flavors collide,
The cravings of shores bring joy worldwide!

## Coconuts and Gentle Breezes

In a hat made of leaves, I drink with glee,
Coconuts wobble, they laugh back at me.
Sand between toes, life's a breezy dance,
Palm trees sway wildly, lost in the chance.

Seagulls complain, dive-bombing my fry,
While crabs gather shells, plotting their sly.
The sun winks and waves, peeking with cheer,
I chuckle and shout, 'Hey, lend me an ear!'

The beach ball escapes, rolling down the sand,
A chase ensues, oh, isn't life grand?
With laughter galore, my heart takes a flight,
In this paradise, everything feels right.

## Tropical Whispers

A mango once whispered, 'Let's have some fun!'
'Oh peach, you're so sly, always on the run!'
Bananas join in, with their jokes on a peel,
They slip on their laughter, it's all a big deal.

Papayas parade, in their bright, silly gear,
They tickle our senses, bringing us cheer.
Pineapples grin, with their crowns held up high,
Spreading the gossip as clouds roll on by.

Each fruit in the bowl, has a story to tell,
Of sun-kissed adventures, both silly and swell.
Beneath neon skies, where the breezes delight,
We dance with the fruit, till the stars shine bright.

## **Nectar of Sunlit Shores**

Sipping the nectar, oh what a delight,
With limes doing cartwheels, they're ready to fight.
Cherries throw confetti, all rosy and sweet,
While oranges juggle, they dance on their feet.

The coconuts giggle, they're light as a breeze,
Buried in laughter, they sway with the trees.
Each splash of the waves, tells jokes on the shore,
The bounty of sunshine leaves us wanting more.

Let's bask in this warmth, where the punchlines flow,
With smoothies and laughs, we steal the show.
In a fruit-filled fiesta, we find blissful scores,
With giggles and joy, on our sunlit shores.

## Paradise in Every Bite

A slice of delight, it's a fruity surprise,
Where pineapples chuckle with mischievous eyes.
Kiwis in sunglasses, they lounge and they chill,
Telling the mango, 'Come on, join the thrill!'

The grapes gossip sweetly, all bundled in cheer,
They bounce on the vine, whispering, 'It's here!'
With plums in the spotlight, they dance in a line,
Proclaiming for all, 'Taste this joy divine!'

From smoothies to sorbets, each nibble a song,
In this carnival of flavors, we all belong.
With laughter and sunshine that brighten our sights,
In every fresh bite, there's pure paradise.

# Vibrance in Every Orchard

In orchards bright, the colors clash,
With fruits that giggle, wiggle, and splash.
Bananas wearing funky shoes,
Pineapples dancing, spreading the news.

Mangoes whisper silly tales,
While coconuts ride on tiny gales.
Limes with hats, lemons in tow,
Fruit fiesta, what a show!

Papayas roll like bowling balls,
Chasing each other in fruity halls.
Grapefruits wear shades, all cool and sly,
Bouncing on branches, oh my, oh my!

In this orchard of joy, all is bright,
Fun-loving fruits that burst with delight.
Come join the party, let's eat and cheer,
Where laughter and flavors ring loud and clear.

## **Sun-Kissed Splendor**

On sunny days, the fruits come out,
With sunglasses on, they laugh and shout.
Watermelons giggle, juice running free,
Strawberries prancing, as sweet as can be.

Peaches cozy in a fuzzy coat,
Cherries jamming on a fruity boat.
Citrus friends are having a ball,
Zesty jokes, they're the life of it all!

Pineapples stand in a spiky line,
Ready to party, feeling just fine.
Each fruit a star, a flavor parade,
In fields of sunshine, let's dance, let's invade!

So grab a slice, won't you join in?
With fruits this merry, where do we begin?
In this sun-kissed land, life's a delight,
Laughter's the fruit that's always just right.

## **Rainforest's Hidden Gem**

Deep in the jungle, a secret hides,
With fruits that giggle and silly slides.
Tropical treasures, a fruity cache,
With monkeys swinging, come join the fray!

Coconuts hang with a cheeky grin,
While dreaming of smoothies they're ready to spin.
Papayas play hide-and-seek in the trees,
With toucans laughing, floating on breeze.

Fruits in pajamas, what a sight!
Dancing with critters in the moonlight.
Each burst of flavor, a comical tune,
In this rainforest, life's a festoon!

So venture here, where the wild things roam,
Where juicy delights feel right at home.
With laughter and sweetness, the jungle's alive,
In this hidden gem, we truly thrive.

## Sugared Nightfall

As night falls down, the fruits start to glow,
With twinkling lights in a sugary show.
Berries in pajamas, all snuggled tight,
Mocking the stars with their fruity delight.

Kiwi comedians crack silly jokes,
While grapes roll in clusters, giggling folks.
Peaches sneak in for a midnight treat,
With flavors that dance, oh what a feat!

Bananas slip under the moon's bright gaze,
Turning their peel into silly plays.
Mangoes twirl in a sugary swirl,
As nighttime wraps them in a fruity whirl.

In this sugary night, laughter's the key,
With fruits so jolly, let's all stay and see.
When moonlight mixes with flavors so sweet,
It's a party of joy, a delicious feat!

## Castaway Delights

On a sandy beach I sit,
With coconuts that wobble a bit.
Mangoes roll like silly clowns,
While pineapples wear fruit crowns.

Papayas dance with glee all day,
Reminding me I'm here to play.
A parrot makes a fruit buffet,
And I just laugh the hours away.

The sun is bright, my shades are wide,
I'm sipping juice, what a wild ride!
Bananas slip, a playful tease,
As I just chuckle in the breeze.

Life's a piña colada dream,
With berries bursting at the seam.
Here in paradise, joy doesn't hide,
With fruity friends, I'll take the ride!

## The Cabana's Culmination

In a cabana full of cheer,
I spot the fruits, oh dear, oh dear!
A watermelon's grin so wide,
Makes every worry run and hide.

Cherries giggle on the vine,
While limes just pout; they're feeling fine.
Coconut drinks with little straws,
Raise my spirits with no cause.

Grapefruits bounce without a care,
Those sneaky oranges beware!
A fruit explosion at noon's peak,
Life's fruity laughter, all we seek.

The sun dips low, the party swells,
With every slice, a tale it tells.
In fruit-filled antics, time does fly,
Who knew bananas could wear a tie?

**Feast from the Tropic's Table**

Gather 'round this festive feast,
With every fruit, a giggle at least.
A feast of flavors, colors parade,
Where laughter's served, and worries fade.

Kiwi wearing glasses so round,
While grapes in bunches tumble down.
A fruit cake jumps—oops, too much rum!
This tropical table's never glum!

Juicy mangoes burst with mirth,
Bananas peel and show their worth.
Strawberries wink in rosy glow,
A playful banquet, oh, let it flow!

As the sun sets, so bright and bold,
The tales of fruit and fun unfold.
With tipsy coconuts all around,
Life's fruity feast is where joy's found!

## The Tropical Cache

I found a treasure chest of glee,
Full of fruits and mystery!
Mangoes whisper sweet and low,
With citrus tales for all to know.

A stash of goodies, what a sight,
With laughing pears on a crazy flight.
Lemons roll like mischievous sprites,
While cherries plan their playful nights.

Ripe avocado diving in style,
Taking the plunge with a big smile.
The cache explodes in rainbow hues,
Dancing flavors, a feast to choose!

As I dig through this wondrous pile,
I can't help but grin all the while.
In the tropical hideaway I crave,
With every fruit, I laugh and wave!

**Ripe Revelations**

In a land where colors cheer,
Bananas slip, oh dear!
Coconuts roll, what a sight,
Falling down, it's quite a fright.

Mangoes dance beneath the sun,
With sticky hands, oh what fun!
Pineapples wear a prickly crown,
Juicy bites, we'll never frown!

Papayas giggle, ripe and sweet,
They love it when you take a bite to eat.
Fruit flies hover, but don't you fret,
They're just here to join the duet!

Limes get squeezed, they twist and shout,
Transforms our drinks, without a doubt.
So grab a slice, don't be shy,
In this fruity world, let's get high!

## Island's Juicy Secrets

On the shore, a coconut smiles,
That's one way to make some miles.
Mangoes wink with a juicy grace,
Sipping nectar at a lively pace.

Tropical fruits gather around,
Creating laughter, the joy profound.
Lychees giggle, so delightfully soft,
While dragon fruit dreams of being loft.

Bananas peel away their pride,
Carrying secrets they can't hide.
Guavas whisper of forbidden cheer,
Join the party, no room for fear!

In this haven where flavors meet,
Grapefruits dancing with light on their feet.
Let's not forget the passionfruit cheer,
Bringing laughter, far and near!

## Nature's Golden Gems

A golden mango sits in style,
With a grin that stretches a mile.
Pineapple crowns wobble in glee,
Saying, "Come on, share with me!"

Watermelons roll, making a splash,
Fruity giggles as they dash.
Cherries blush, adorning the cake,
With one little bite, oh what a wake!

A fig winks, filled with sweet, sweet charm,
Whispering wishes to disarm.
While oranges juggle their juicy fate,
Let's raise a toast and celebrate!

Durian's smell, it's quite the beast,
Yet its flavor's a savory feast.
Together we laugh at nature's whims,
These golden gems, oh how they brim!

## Savoring Summer's Embrace

In the sun, a treasure awaits,
Squeezed lemon joins the plates.
Citrus giggles, so tangy and bright,
Each zesty bite feels just right.

Limes twist and dance in the breeze,
Tickling our noses with playful tease.
The sweet scent of ripe bananas,
Invites us to join the piranhas!

Papaya nudges with a friendly push,
While starfruit shines, making a fuss.
Soursop grins with its own flair,
In this fruity world, we have no care!

So let's savor summer's embrace,
With every fruit, let's pick up the pace.
Laughing together, under the sun,
In this fruity paradise, we have won!

## Whirl of Fruit and Flavor

In breezy markets, colors collide,
A pineapple winks, says, "Come take a ride!"
Mangoes juggle, dancing on stands,
While coconuts giggle; they're in high demand.

Bananas split like comedians on stage,
Limes squirt jokes, it's all the rage!
Papayas do pirouettes, so divine,
In this fruity circus, oh how they shine!

Pomegranates pop like party balloons,
With each juicy bite, laughter attunes.
Tropical treats, a vibrant affair,
Join the feast, come have a share!

What a spectacle, this fruity brigade,
In every corner, a joyous charade.
So dive right in, no need to be coy,
In this festival of flavor, bring your joy!

## Bouncing Blues and Fire-Engine Reds

Blueberries bounce on their tiny feet,
While strawberries shout, "We're the sweetest treat!"
Cherries do cartwheels, red as a blaze,
This fruity fiesta, a riot of praise!

Watermelons splash like kids in the sun,
Raspberries giggle, having such fun.
Kiwis spin tales, fuzzy and bright,
With laughter echoing into the night.

Peaches get sassy, they know they're the best,
While lemons look sharp, never to rest.
In this carnival, chaos reigns free,
With every vibrant hue, just let it be!

Let's dance with the rhythm of juicy delights,
In the heart of summer, where flavor ignites.
So grab a bowl, let laughter extend,
In this fun fruit jamboree, it never ends!

## Every Bite a Story

Each slice reveals a tale to unfold,
From a sweet little mango, adventures untold.
Pineapples whisper of sunny shores,
As oranges giggle, opening their doors.

Biting a lychee, you unleash a thrill,
A burst of laughter, a flavor to fill.
Dragonfruit dreams in vibrant display,
With every munch, we shout hooray!

Bananas plot mischief, peeling with flair,
While passion fruits spill secrets to share.
A history in each precious seed,
Dive into bites, it's a fruity creed!

So come gather round, let stories collide,
In this tasty journey, let joy be your guide.
Each juicy moment, a giggle in disguise,
With every delicious bite, hear laughter arise!

## Colors of Paradise on the Palate

A palette of colors, a feast for the eyes,
Tropical hues wearing fruit disguise.
From bright flamingo pinks to sunset gold,
These tasty delights have stories to told.

Kumquats twirl with zest, making us laugh,
While blueberries plot in their juicy craft.
Grapefruits sip cocktails, oh what a scene,
In this fruity paradise, life feels so keen!

Peppers dance spicy in vibrant green,
While bananas are clowns in their bright, sunny sheen.
Come take a bite, let the laughter flow,
For paradise lives in every tasty show!

So taste the colors, embrace every shade,
In this carnival of flavor, let worries evade.
In every juicy morsel, happiness stays,
As we celebrate life in the funnest ways!

www.ingramcontent.com/pod-product-compliance
Lightning Source LLC
Chambersburg PA
CBHW072217070526
44585CB00015B/1384